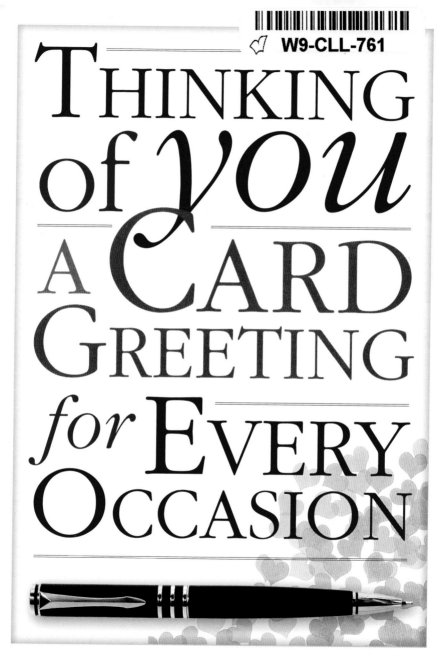

THINKING of *you*
A CARD
GREETING
for EVERY
OCCASION

ANNIVERSARIES • VALENTINE'S DAY • MOTHER'S DAY • FATHER'S DAY

THINKING of *you*

A CARD GREETING *for* EVERY OCCASION

h
hinkler

Published by Hinkler Books Pty Ltd
45–55 Fairchild Street
Heatherton Victoria 3202 Australia
www.hinkler.com.au

hinkler

© Hinkler Books Pty Ltd 2010, 2016

Author: Katie Hewat
Design: Sam Grimmer
Typesetting: MPS Limited

Images © Shutterstock.com: Bouquet of flowers © BelleMedia; Alpamayo peak
© Galyna Andrushko; Teddy bear with rose © Ooi Sze Erh; A man proposing
© Phase4Photography; Silver champagne © Sandra Cunningham;
Graduation cap © Anyka; Hand holding a four leaf clover © Jozsef Szasz-Fabian;
Family day © Carlos Gauna; Agenda © Kuzma; Three beautiful red roses
© Stephanie Frey; White waterlily © Darkpurple; Baby booties © Ruth Black;
Daisies © Mary Rice; Hearts © nito; Black ballpoint pen © Robyn Mackenzie;
Beautiful gift box © Denis Vrublevski; Four glass balls © Ariene; Gold pen
© Ambient Ideas.

ISBN: 978 1 4889 0557 5

Printed and bound in China

CONTENTS

INTRODUCTION

What is
uttered
from the heart alone,
Will win the
hearts
of others to your
own.

Johann Wolfgang von Goethe

THE BENEFITS OF GIVING GREETING CARDS

Giving a greeting card to someone not only provides a huge emotional benefit to the receiver, it can also be a rewarding experience for the giver. It helps us feel connected to people, happy that we have helped to brighten someone's day.

Receiving a greeting card makes us feel important, loved and closer to those who take the time to convey these small gestures. It can certainly help to personalise a gift we have given to or received from someone, though often a few words of respect, sympathy or joy can be enough on their own.

Expressing how we feel about others can sometimes be difficult, and greeting cards provide us with a means of doing this personally and privately.

They can help someone through a time of grief or hardship, boost their high spirits during times of achievement or just let them know someone is thinking of them on those special days. Greeting cards also provide a keepsake that people can hold on to and use to reflect on the past and feel closer to the people that matter to them.

THE IMPORTANCE OF CONVEYING SINCERITY

When purchasing a greeting card for a friend or loved one, quite often the words written inside don't do justice to what we want to say. This is why sometimes it's important to add a personal message as well. The message should come straight from the heart – it's not often we get the chance to tell the people we care about exactly what they mean to us.

Think about how many times you have received a greeting card that just said a basic 'to you, from me'. Now compare that with the cards you have received that contained heartfelt messages. Quite a big difference, isn't it?

People know whether what they are reading is sincere, which is why it is important to make the message as

personalised and relevant as possible.
It's no use listing wonderful qualities that
you admire in a person if those qualities
are not really evident. Using personal
anecdotes can be a great way to make
your messages meaningful.

Remember the one most important rule
when writing your message: don't be afraid
to tell people how much you care.

THE EMERGENCE OF THE GREETING CARD

We all know that giving or sending greeting cards is a simple and effective way of staying in touch and reaching out to those we care about, but where did the greeting card come from?

As far as we know, the first civilisation to employ the use of greeting cards was the ancient Chinese, who used them for the purpose of conveying New Year's wishes.

The earliest paper greeting card in existence is a Valentine's Day card that originated in Germany during the 1400s. It now resides in the British Museum.

The development of better printing methods and the introduction of postage stamps saw the greeting card become

less costly and, therefore, reach new heights of popularity during the 1840s. Since then the greeting card has become commonplace, with roughly 7 billion cards selling each year in the US alone.

Modern Technology

With the emergence of technology such as the telegraph, fax machines and now the internet, letter writing has become obsolete and many people opt to send electronic cards and correspondence to save time, money and resources.

Other easy methods of keeping in touch have materialised in recent years, including online social networks such as Instagram and Facebook, blogging, SMS and even Twitter. But even though many of us have been able to build their everyday use into our busy lives, it just isn't the same; the joy of receiving a hand-written letter or card has always remained.

TIPS FOR STAYING CONNECTED TO FRIENDS AND LOVED ONES

Sometimes it's not as easy as it would seem to stay connected to people we value. You might like to consider some of the following tips for maintaining positive communication in those relationships.

- Consider making time each day or week to reach out to the people you care about, whether through phone calls, messages or cards. With the busy lives we all lead, it can be easy for months or years to pass while we're thinking, 'I'll call tomorrow'.

- Remember there doesn't need to be a good reason for you to contact friends and family. A quick note or card saying 'Thinking of you' or a phone call will always be appreciated.

- It can be really easy for small misunderstandings, uncertainties or disagreements to turn into something far bigger. A simple message saying 'sorry' when you have made a mistake or a card saying 'I miss you' can be all it takes to stop these molehills from turning into mountains.

- Think very carefully about what makes you happy when it comes to interaction with your friends and family and try to replicate these actions.

- Hold on to the special messages and cards you receive, as they will help you to reflect on your relationship as time goes by.

- Remember that good friends and relatives support each other. Don't contact people *only* when you have something to celebrate or news to share, make sure you contact them at other times, too. Let them know that you care about how they are and what they are up to, even though you might not have much to tell them.

Using this Book

Many people find it hard to know where to begin when writing messages to friends and loved ones. This book contains quotations and messages to give you inspiration when you set out to write your own message. You may be lucky enough to find exactly what you want to convey in your card straight away, but generally you will need to search through the messages and quotations in each section and take parts of or inspiration from the ones that suit your purpose.

There is a range of styles and types of messages and quotations in each section, which are intended to cover a whole range of situations and purposes. Many of the messages list specific personality traits or events or are targeted at specific people, such as a parent or a friend.

Just remember that you can take any part of any message and make it your own – you might find that a message in the birthday section is suited to what you want to say to your mum on Mother's Day, or one of the wedding messages is more suited to your friend's engagement card. By all means, pick the messages apart and put them back together to say exactly what it is you want to say.

BIRTHDAYS

It takes a long time to grow young.

Pablo Picasso

GENERAL

Have a wonderful birthday! We hope today
is just the beginning of a year
full of happiness.

———•———

Remember: you'll only be this old for one
year, but you'll be fabulous forever! Happy
birthday to a wonderful friend.

———•———

Birthdays are a time to reflect on the
memories of yesterday, the joys of today and
the dreams of tomorrow. Congratulations on
another year of accomplishments.
Have a wonderful day!

———•———

Life has been so crazy lately that I missed
the most important day of the year . . . your
birthday! I hope you had a wonderful day
full of love and laughter.

Happy birthday, [name]! May your day
be filled with friends, family, love and
laughter. You deserve it!

———

May your birthday be every
bit as magnificent as you are! Hope
you have a fabulous day.

———

Happy birthday! May your day be filled with
happiness and your year with joy.

———

Happy birthday! May today bring
every little thing your heart desires . . .
and all the big things, too.

———

We're sending you a very
special birthday wish for a wonderful
day full of joy and laughter, hugs and kisses.
Happy birthday!

Happy birthday! May this day be
just the beginning of a year filled
with happy memories, wonderful moments
and lots of laughs.

———•———

The years have shown kindness
to you in the way that you have always
shown kindness to those around you.
Have a truly wonderful birthday.

———•———

Happiness is living well, laughing often,
loving greatly. Wishing you another year of
happiness. Have a great birthday!

For Partners

Thinking of you with love on your birthday.
I hope today brings you everything that
makes you smile today and always.

———•———

Happy birthday, [name]! I am so glad
to be here sharing this day with you, my
favourite person in the world.

———•———

I have never loved you more than
I do today, but after all of these years
I have learned one thing: I will love you
even more with each and every tomorrow.
Happy birthday!

———•———

Every year you make me just that little bit
prouder, feel just a little bit stronger, and
love you just that little bit more. I didn't
think it was possible. I hope you have
a wonderful birthday filled with all the
happiness you so deserve.

I cannot fix on the hour, or the spot, or the look, or the words, which laid the foundation. It is too long ago. I was in the middle before I had begun.

Jane Austen, Pride and Prejudice

A BIRTHDAY

*My heart is like a singing bird
Whose nest is in a watered shoot;
My heart is like an apple tree
Whose boughs are bent with thickset fruit;
My heart is like a rainbow shell
That paddles in a halcyon sea;
My heart is gladder than all these
Because my love is come to me.*

Christina Rossetti

My heroes are my parents. I can't think of having anyone else as my heroes.

Michael Jordan

For Parents

Happy birthday, [Mum/Dad]! Thank you so much for always being there for me. The love, support, care and inspiration you have given me are what have made me the person I am today. I hope you have a wonderful day filled with all the happiness you deserve.

———•———

Have a wonderful birthday, [Mum/Dad]! Enjoy this special day that belongs just to you. You have earned it.

———•———

Happy birthday, [Mum/Dad]! On this very special day, we just wanted to say thank you so much for being the wonderful [mum/dad] that you are – we could never have wished for anyone better.

———•———

Thank you for being my parent, my nurse, my coach, my teacher and my friend. I hope that today will be every bit as special as you are. Happy birthday!

For Children

Happy birthday little one! I hope your special day is filled with hugs, laughter and surprises.

———•———

Today we celebrate the day you came into the world and changed our lives. You've made us so happy and so very proud. Happy birthday!

———•———

Happy birthday, [name]! I can't believe you're [age] already! I hope your magical day is full of fun and all your birthday wishes come true.

———•———

Best wishes for a bright and beautiful birthday to a bright and beautiful little [boy/girl].

———•———

Wow – a whole year older! Wishing you the biggest, bestest, funnest birthday ever!

Milestone Birthdays

[18/21] years ago I held you in my arms and thought I could never be prouder. But on this day you enter the world as a strong, intelligent, honest and passionate [man/woman], and it is truly the proudest day of my life. Happy birthday.

———•———

Happy 30th birthday! Remember: the more candles you have, the bigger the wish you're allowed! May all your dreams and wishes come true on this very exciting day.

———•———

Happy 40th birthday! You have now finally reached that age where you can begin to enjoy life with confidence and a new-found sense of freedom. Best wishes for a wonderful birthday and many more to come!

Sing, dance, eat, play: remember, you're never too old to have fun! Happy 50th birthday!

———•———

Happy 60th birthday! Today is a celebration of you who are, what you've done, the things you have achieved and what you've overcome. But most of all, it's a celebration of all the great experiences that still lie ahead. Have a sensational day.

———•———

Happy 70th birthday to a person who is very wise, a person who we all look up to and admire, a person who is respected by all, a person who provides inspiration to those around [him/her] every day. May your day be filled with every imaginable joy.

———•———

Happy 80th birthday to a truly wonderful person who never fails to greet each new day with wonder in [his/her] eyes and kindness in [his/her] heart. Our very best wishes for a wonderful day.

WEDDINGS

Now join your hands, and with your hands your hearts...

William Shakespeare

FOR FAMILY

Welcome to our family, [name]. Thank you for bringing such joy into our [wonderful son's/ beautiful daughter's] life and making [him/ her] so happy. We look forward to watching the two of you grow as you build your lives together and we'll be there to love and support you every step of the way. We are so very proud of you both. Congratulations.

———•———

Congratulations on your wedding. This is one of the proudest days of our lives and we will all treasure the memories for a lifetime. We feel truly blessed to have such a wonderful [son/daughter] and [daughter-in-law/ son-in-law]. We love you with all of our hearts and can't wait to see what the future will bring for you both.

Congratulations on your wedding! You have built your lives together over many years, created a loving and happy home and grown into amazing people, of whom we are immensely proud. We are truly overjoyed that you are taking this next big step in your lives. We wish you all the happiness in the world in the years to come.

To the bride and groom, two of the people we love most in this world. We are so proud to be here with you on this amazing day, and we feel blessed that we have a new [brother/sister-in-law] to welcome into our family. We look forward to sharing in your bright and happy future.

Ring sweetest bells, in merry peals,
Ring for the love the eye reveals,
Ring for the vows that make two one,
Ring for the best day 'neath the sun.

Traditional English rhyme

Love is that condition in which the happiness
of another person is essential to your own.

Robert A. Heinlein

Everything that touches us, me and you,
takes us together like a violin's bow,
which draws one voice out of two separate strings.
Upon what instrument are we two spanned?
And what musician holds us in his hand?
Oh sweetest song.

Rainer Marie Rilke, from Love Song,
translated by Stephen Mitchell

Chains do not hold a marriage together. It is threads, hundreds of tiny threads which sew people together through the years.

Simone Signoret

The groom always smiles proudly because he's convinced he's accomplished something quite wonderful. The bride smiles because she's been able to convince him of it.

Judith McNaught

'I won't believe you're married till I see the bishop and assistant clergy mopping their foreheads and saying, "Well, that's that. We've really got the young blighter off at last."'

P.G. Wodehouse, **Aunts Aren't Gentlemen**

FOR FRIENDS

Best wishes for a beautiful life to two of
life's most beautiful people. May the coming
years be filled with love, laughter and
happiness. We're so very proud of you
both. Congratulations!

———•———

In all the years that we have been friends, I've
never seen you as happy as you are when
you are with [name]. You are two of the most
amazing, warm and caring people I have ever
known, and I hope this day brings you all the
joy and happiness you could ever wish for.

———•———

May your future be filled with good health,
happiness and lots of hugs and kisses.
Congratulations on your wedding day.

———•———

Congratulations on the first day of your
wonderful partnership through life. Enjoy this
special moment and always remember that
the love you share is truly a beautiful thing.

To the bride and groom, the two happiest people on Earth, may you always have delight in your hearts and love in your home. Best wishes for a wonderful future together.

———•———

May you continue to be each other's best friend and together fill your lives with fun, love and laughter. Wishing you a lifetime full of wonderful tomorrows.

———•———

Here's to a new home, a new beginning and a new life for you both. Wishing you all the happiness you so deserve on your wedding day.

———•———

You have both been blessed with the miraculous gift of finding your one true soul mate. We know that you will fill each other's hearts with joy and happiness for the rest of your lives together. Congratulations!

Who **marries** *for* love *without* **money** has good *nights* and **sorry** days.

English proverb

Let us celebrate the occasion with wine
and sweet words.

Plautus

———•———

And as this round
Is nowhere found
To flaw, or else to sever,
So let our love
As endless prove
And pure as gold forever.

Robert Herrick

———•———

Love thy wife as thyself; honour her more
than thyself. He who lives unmarried lives
without joy.

The Talmud

Thank you so much for inviting us to share this wonderful day. You're both so lucky to have found that one special person you want to be with every day for the rest of your lives – and may every one of those days be just as happy as this one. Congratulations.

It is a true privilege to be here on this momentous occasion and to be able to share it with two such deserving people. You both work so hard to brighten the lives of those around you and it is wonderful to see you enjoying this day that is entirely yours. Savour every moment!

Congratulations on your wedding day. Yours is a marriage built on the most important of foundations: love, trust, loyalty, respect and friendship. We know that you will live long, happy lives and, together, make all your greatest dreams come true.

We are so very excited for the both of you
as you start out on this wonderful journey.
We wish you luck, success and, most of
all, happiness for all the years to come.
Congratulations!

———•———

Congratulations! What could be more fulfilling
than standing before your friends and family
and making the commitment to become
husband and wife. You will always look back
on this day with warmth and joy, but I'm
sure it is only the beginning of the wonderful
things life has in store for you both.

———•———

Best wishes for a lifetime filled with
sunny smiles, warm hugs and laughter.
Congratulations on this special day.

———•———

We've always known this day would
come, and we're so very happy to be here
sharing it with you. If ever there were two
people meant for each other, it is you.
Congratulations and best wishes to you both.

A marriage makes of two fractional lines a whole; it gives two purposeless lives a work, and doubles the strength of each to perform it; it gives to two questioning natures a reason for living and something to live for.

Mark Twain

She who dwells with me,
Whom I have loved with such communion,
That no place on earth
Can ever be a solitude to me.

William Blake

Now you will feel no rain, for each of you will be shelter for the other. Now you will feel no cold, for each of you will be warmth to the other. Now there will be no loneliness, for each of you will be companion to the other. Now you are two persons, but there is only one life before you. May beauty surround you both in the journey ahead and through all the years. May happiness be your companion and may your days together be good and long upon this earth.

Apache wedding blessing,
translator unknown

WEDLOCK'S CHARMS

As Roses other flowers excel
So Wedlock's charm still wears the bell
Among the joys of human life.
No pleasure can with these compare
Which faithful love alone can share
Twixt happy man and wife.

Author unknown

May all the joy and happiness you have brought to those around you be returned a thousandfold on this glorious day and all of the days that follow. Thank you for being such wonderful friends and for allowing us to share this special occasion with you both.

———•———

Congratulations to the bride and groom! I'm sure that, together, you will build a warm and happy home and a wonderful life.

———•———

Congratulations on your wedding day. May your lives together be a grand adventure in which you face foes and overcome obstacles side by side. Together you can accomplish anything!

———•———

Congratulations on your wedding. We wish you all the very best for your future life together. Sorry that we couldn't make it there to share the day with you.

It is easy for everyone to see that the two of you were made for each other. Live, laugh, dance, eat and enjoy every day that you have, for to meet one's soul mate is truly a blessing. Wishing all the happiness in the world to you both.

———•———

Congratulations on your wedding. We wish you a wonderful life together as husband and wife. May the happiness of this day last a lifetime.

———•———

What an amazing thing to be able to completely and wholly share your life with another person – a person who will always be there to double your joys and halve your sorrows. Here's to a wonderful life together.

———•———

Warmest congratulations to you both on your wedding day. We are so sorry we couldn't be there to share this special day, but we are thinking of you and wish you all the happiness in the world. You deserve it.

ENGAGEMENTS

Whatever our souls are made of, his and mine are the same...

Emily Brontë

For Family

Congratulations on your engagement!
We've all been hoping that this day would
come and we're so very happy that
you have decided to spend the rest of
your lives together.

―――

We're so very proud of you both
and we couldn't be happier that you've
decided to take this step. We look forward
to watching you build a wonderful life
together. Congratulations.

―――

Seeing how happy the two of you are when
you are together, there can be no doubt that
this was meant to be. Congratulations on
your engagement and all our very best for a
long, happy and healthy life together.

Congratulations to you both at this very special time. We could not be more excited to be welcoming a new [brother/sister] into our family and we know the two of you will continue to make each other very happy.

———•———

We have never been prouder than we are today on the day of your engagement. The way that you look at each other and take care of each other really is a joy to see. Congratulations.

———•———

I have never seen a couple more happy, more caring or more in love than the two of you. I look forward more than anything to being there on the big day to see you finally tie the knot. Congratulations on your engagement.

Marriage

is a sort of

friendship

recognised

by the

police.

Robert Louis Stevenson

It is a wonderful advantage to a man, in every pursuit of avocation, to secure an adviser in a sensible woman . . . A man's best friend is a wife of good sense and good heart who loves him.

Edward Bulwer-Lytton

———•———

Two things do prolong thy life,
A quiet heart and a loving wife.

Author unknown

———•———

What greater thing is there for two human souls than to feel that they are joined . . . to be at one with each other in silent, unspeakable memories.

George Eliot

For Friends

Congratulations on your engagement! Planning to spend the rest of your lives together is cause for celebration. Enjoy every moment as you begin this very exciting journey.

As you grow old together, may the love you share for each other remain as young and vibrant as it is today. Congratulations on your engagement.

Falling in love is the most wonderful gift life has to offer. May your engagement be just the beginning of a life together full of wonder, warmth and laughter. Congratulations.

For a successful wedding you need a date, a dress, some flowers and a location. For a successful marriage you need love, trust, friendship and the ability to compromise. We know that you will find success in both. Congratulations on your engagement.

As you begin on this, one of life's great journeys, may you enjoy each other's quirks, accept each other's differences, laugh at your arguments, trust your hearts and forever be in love. Congratulations on your engagement.

———•———

We were very excited to hear of your engagement – no two people in the world deserve happiness more than you. Congratulations.

———•———

Congratulations on your engagement! May every new day be even brighter than the one before as you take this first step towards a long and happy marriage.

———•———

Congratulations on your engagement. You really are a beautiful couple and we are so glad that we could be here sharing this special day with you both.

If it weren't for the presents, an elopement would be preferable.

George Ade

The ring is on my hand
And the wreath is on my brow,
Satins and jewels grand
Are all at my command
And I am happy now.

Edgar Allan Poe

The minute I heard my first love story
I started looking for you, not knowing
how blind that was.
Lovers don't finally meet somewhere.
They're in each other all along.

Rumi, translated by Coleman Barks
with John Moyne

We're so very excited for you both! Making such a strong commitment to one another brings about heightened feelings of happiness, stability, trust, confidence and respect. Being married to the one you love is the greatest feeling in the world. Congratulations on deciding to take this big step.

———•———

Congratulations on your engagement. How exciting – a long, happy and wonderful future to look forward to! Enjoy this special day and all of those that follow.

———•———

Love each other, respect each other and you will be happy. It really is as simple as that. Congratulations on your engagement and we wish you both a lifetime of happiness.

———•———

Congratulations on your engagement. We are so very happy for you both and we feel honoured to be sharing this day with you.

May every happiness be yours on this joyous occasion and every day hereafter. Congratulations.

———•———

Thank you for inviting us to celebrate this wonderful occasion. Congratulations on your engagement and here's wishing you a life together full of wonder, love and laughter.

———•———

Congratulations to two amazing people who deserve a lifetime of happiness. We were so excited to hear about your engagement and we look forward to being there to share the big day with you.

ANNIVERSARIES

Love
is something
eternal;
the aspect may change,
but not the
essence.

Vincent van Gogh

GENERAL

Happy anniversary to a wonderful couple. Watching the two of you together makes anything seem possible.

———•———

The two of you are the perfect example of how a couple should live together, laugh together and love one another. Happy anniversary!

———•———

Happy 50th anniversary to two very dear friends. May your golden wedding anniversary be filled with joyous memories and new adventures.

———•———

May the moon shine and the stars sparkle just for the two of you tonight. Happy anniversary.

On this special day, we wish you love, laughter and happiness in your lives and thank you for those very things that your friendship brings into ours. Happy anniversary.

———

Happy anniversary to an amazing couple. The love and happiness you share is an inspiration to those around you. Congratulations.

———

Happy anniversary! A lasting marriage is a joy to those who are part of it as well as to those who love them. Wishing you both every happiness today and in all the years to come. Congratulations!

———

Happy anniversary! Today is a celebration of all the dreams you have made come true, and all those that still lie ahead. We wish all the happiness in the world to two people who sincerely deserve it.

Love creates an 'us' without destroying the 'me'.

Leo Buscaglia

Once the realization is accepted
that even between the closest people
infinite distances exist, a marvellous living
side-by-side can grow up for them, if they
succeed in loving the expanse between
them, which gives them the possibility
of always seeing each other as a whole
and before an immense sky.

Rainer Marie Rilke, from **Letters,**
translated by Stephen Mitchell

Come live with me and be my Love,
And we will all the pleasures prove
That hills and valley, dales and fields,
Or woods or sleepy mountain yields.

Christopher Marlowe

FOR PARTNERS

Each and every day you make me feel like
the luckiest [man/woman] in the world.
Happy anniversary, my love.

———•———

To my wonderful [husband/wife], I wish
there were words enough to explain how
very much I love you. Thank you for making
every day a treasured memory. Happy
anniversary.

———•———

It seems like just yesterday that we stood
before our family and friends and made our
promises to love each other for the rest of
our lives. Thank you for making the last
[number] years the happiest of my life. I just
can't wait to see what exciting adventures
the future has in store for us. Happy
anniversary.

Love is a symbol of eternity. It wipes out all sense of time, destroying all memory of a beginning and all fear of an end.

Madame de Stael

All love at first, like generous wine,
Ferments and frets until 'tis fine;
But when 'tis settled on the lee,
And from th'impurer matter free,
Becomes the richer still, the older,
And proves the pleasanter the colder.

Samuel Butler

Love is what you've been through
with somebody.

James Thurber

Time is
Too slow for those who wait,
Too swift for those who fear,
Too long for those who grieve,
Too short for those who rejoice,
But for those who love, time is Eternity.
Hours fly; flowers die;
New days, new ways, pass by.
Love stays.

Henry van Dyke

I look back on our years together with fondness and joy and forward to our future together with excitement and expectation. Thank you for being everything a [man/woman] could possibly hope for in a [husband/wife]. Happy anniversary.

Thank you for giving me a beautiful home, a beautiful life and a beautiful family to love. You make me so very proud to be your wife. Happy anniversary.

Happy anniversary! Thank you for always making me feel beautiful, special and, most of all, loved. I treasure the memories of the years we have spent together and look forward to creating many more.

A SECOND WEDDING RING

'Thee, Mary, with this ring I wed,'
So fourteen years ago, I said.
Behold another ring! 'For what?'
To wed thee o'er again – why not?

With that first ring I married youth,
Grace, beauty, innocence and truth;
Taste long admired, sense long revered,
And all my Mary then appeared.

If she, by merit since disclosed,
Prove twice the woman I supposed,
I plead that double merit now,
To justify a double vow.

Samuel Bishop

Partnership,
not
dependence,
is the
real romance
in
marriage.

Muriel Fox

For Parents and Grandparents

Congratulations on your [number] anniversary. Your marriage is the foundation on which our entire family was built; your children and grandchildren have grown up feeling secure in the stability and support that comes from the love you have for your family and each other. Here's to many more happy years together.

———•———

Mum and Dad, congratulations on another year of marriage, and thank you for another year of unconditional love and support. You both deserve all the happiness in the world. Happy anniversary.

———•———

Congratulations on another year of a happy, loving and supportive marriage. I consider myself truly blessed to have been given two such wonderful people as my parents. Happy anniversary.

What an amazing accomplishment: to build a happy marriage, to create a warm and loving home, to raise a wonderful family and to do it all together, hand in hand. You are both truly an inspiration and we feel very lucky to have grown up knowing the love of two such very special people. Happy anniversary.

Happy anniversary, [Mum and Dad/Grandma and Grandpa]! It warms my heart to see the way the two of you still care for each other and it is a wonderful thing to know that we never grow too old for holding hands.

Story writers say that love is concerned only with young people and the excitement and glamour of romance end at the altar. How blind they are. The best romance is inside marriage: the finest love stories come after the wedding, not before.

Irving Stone

Love seems the swiftest, but it is the slowest of all growths. No man or woman knows what perfect love is until they have been married for a quarter of a century.

Mark Twain

WEDDING ANNIVERSARY GIFTS

First year	*Paper*
Second year	*Cotton*
Third year	*Leather*
Fourth year	*Flowers*
Fifth year	*Wood*
Sixth year	*Iron*
Seventh year	*Copper*
Eighth year	*Bronze*
Ninth year	*Pottery*
Tenth year	*Aluminium*
Eleventh year	*Steel*
Twelfth year	*Silk*
Thirteenth year	*Lace*
Fourteenth year	*Ivory*
Fifteenth year	*Crystal glass*
Twentieth year	*China*
Thirtieth year	*Pearl*
Fortieth year	*Ruby*
Forty-fifth year	*Sapphire*
Fiftieth year	*Gold*
Fifty-fifth year	*Emerald*
Sixtieth year	*Diamond*

BABIES

A babe
in the house is a
well-spring of
pleasure,
a messenger of
peace and love,
a resting place for
innocence
on earth,
a link between
angels and men.

Martin Farquhar Tupper

A New Baby

We have been looking forward to meeting little [name] for such a long time and we are so excited that [he/she] is finally here. [He/she] has brought joy into all of our hearts and we know that [he/she] will make you just as proud of [him/her] as you have made us each and every day of your life.

———

We are overjoyed at the arrival of our new [grandson/granddaughter, name], and we know that the two of you will provide [him/her] with all the love and happiness that any child could wish for. We are so proud of you both.

———

To the sweetest little [niece/nephew] that an aunt and uncle could hope for, we welcome you into our family with all of our hearts and look forward to playing with you, laughing with you and watching you grow.

Congratulations on the safe arrival of little [name]. [He/she] is the perfect addition to your perfect family.

———•———

Such wonderful news that [name] has finally arrived! [He/she] is truly blessed to be a part of your warm and loving family. We look forward to meeting [him/her] soon. Congratulations.

———•———

Sometimes the smallest things bring the greatest joys. Congratulations on the arrival of your baby [boy/girl].

———•———

How wonderful – a new baby [boy/girl] to love. We're so very happy for you both and wish you a lifetime of joy as you watch [him/her] laugh, learn and grow.

———•———

There is no greater love than that which exists between a parent and their child. We wish your new family all the joy that only a new baby can bring.

A baby is born with a need to be loved –
and never outgrows it.

Frank A. Clark

The only creatures that are evolved enough
to convey pure love are dogs and infants.

Johnny Depp

Sometimes when you pick up your child you
can feel a map of your bones beneath your
hands, or smell the scent of your own skin
in the nape of his neck.

Jodi Picoult, Perfect Match

Of all the joys that brighten suffering earth, What joy is welcom'd like a newborn child!

Caroline Norton

[Name] is a very lucky little [boy/girl] to be given two such wonderful parents. We know you will be there to praise [him/her] when [he/she] achieves, pick [him/her] up when [he/she] falls and, above all, love [him/her] always and unconditionally. Congratulations.

———

A new baby in your arms, and a new love in all of our hearts. Congratulations on the birth of your [son/daughter].

———

We were overjoyed to hear of the recent arrival of [name]. Congratulations to the proud parents.

———

Parenthood brings so many joys, but none will be greater than the first time you see your little one smile. Congratulations on the birth of your new baby [boy/girl].

Congratulations to you both on the newest addition to your beautiful family. Best wishes for a happy future to you all.

———•———

A new little person to make your family complete! We wish you both and little [name] all the health and happiness in the world.

———•———

Congratulations on one of life's greatest accomplishments – creating a new life. We know that you guys have everything it takes to give [him/her] a wonderful home and help [him/her] grow into an amazing person.

———•———

Congratulations on the arrival of little [name]. We're sure that [he/she] has inherited your fighting spirit and will be home with you very soon. We so look forward to meeting [him/her].

A CRADLE SONG

Sweet dreams, form a shade
O'er my lovely infant's head!
Sweet dreams of pleasant streams
By happy, silent moony beams!

Sweet sleep, with soft down
Weave thy brows an infant crown!
Sweet Sleep, angel mild,
Hover o'er my happy child!

Sweet smiles, in the night
Hover over my delight!
Sweet smiles, mother's smiles,
All the livelong night beguiles.

Sweet moans, dovelike sighs
Chase not slumber from thine eyes!
Sweet moans, sweeter smiles,
All the dovelike moans beguiles.

William Blake

Every babe
born
into the
world
is a finer one
than the last.

Charles Dickens

CHRISTENINGS

We wish you many blessings on
your Christening day and every
day thereafter.

———•———

Congratulations on your [son/daughter's]
Christening. You must be immensely
proud of your little one on this very
special day.

———•———

May the Christening of your child find [him/
her] surrounded by love and happiness.

———•———

Thank you very much for inviting us
to be a part of [name]'s Christening. We wish
you all the greatest joy on this very
special occasion.

They always smell of bread and butter.

Lord Byron

———•———

I'd been handed twenty odd years in this
bundle, and hoped to see her grow, learn
to totter, to run into the garden, run back,
and call this place home. But I realised
from these beginnings that I'd got a daughter
whose life was already separate from
mine . . . She was a child of herself and
would be what she was, I was merely the
keeper of her temporary helplessness.

Laurie Lee

———•———

Standing by the crib of one's own baby,
with that world-old pang of compassion and
protectiveness toward this so little creature
that has all its course to run, the heart flies
back in yearning and gratitude to those who
felt just so toward one's self.

Christopher Morley

A **baby** is an

inestimable

blessing

and

bother.

Mark Twain

It is a joy and a privilege to be here today to take part in [name]'s Christening. [He/she] will grow up knowing that my guidance and support of [him/her] will be there whenever [he/she] needs it.

———•———

We wish you many blessings on this, your Christening day. May your life be filled with faith, love, hope and peace today and always.

———•———

May the love of God guide you through life's journey. Congratulations on your Christening.

———•———

Congratulations on the Christening of your [son/daughter, name]. May the blessings of God be with you today and always.

———•———

May God smile down on your family on this wonderful occasion and for every day of your lives. Congratulations on the Christening of your [son/daughter].

VALENTINE'S DAY

You know
you're in love
when you can't fall asleep
because
reality
is finally
better than your
dreams.

Dr Seuss

For New Partners

I just wanted to let you know that the days spent with you have been the happiest of my life. I hope we can share many more. Happy Valentine's Day.

———◆———

You're funny, you're smart, you're strong, you're sweet; you fill my days with happiness. How could I ever help but fall in love with you?

———◆———

You're my first thought when I wake up every morning, my last thought before I close my eyes at night, and you fill every moment in between. You are the most beautiful person I have ever met and I feel so lucky to have you in my life.

I love who you are and the way you make
me feel when we're together. Thank you for
being mine. Happy Valentine's Day.

———•———

I knew you were the one from the very first
time I laid eyes on you. You mean the whole
world to me and I'm so glad that we're
together. Happy Valentine's Day.

———•———

You're the sweetest Valentine a [guy/girl]
could ever hope for. When we're together
I feel like I can do anything – I love you.

———•———

The day you came into my life you made
me the luckiest [man/woman] in the world.
You're the best thing that has ever happened
to me. Happy Valentine's Day.

———•———

Happy Valentine's Day! I love you
so very much and I hope we can always be
by each other's side, holding hands
and sharing our dreams.

HOW DO I LOVE THEE?

How do I love thee? Let me count the ways.
I love thee to the depth and breadth and height
My soul can reach, when feeling out of sight
For the ends of Being and ideal Grace.
I love thee to the level of every day's
Most quiet need, by sun and candlelight.
I love thee freely as men strive for Right;
I love thee purely, as they turn from Praise.
I love thee with the passion put to use
In my old griefs, and with my childhood's faith.
I love thee with a love I seemed to lose
With my lost saints, – I love thee with the breath,
Smiles, tears, of all my life! – and if God choose,
I shall but love thee better after death.

Elizabeth Barrett Browning

It is best to love wisely, no doubt.
But to love foolishly is better than not to
be able to love at all.

William Makepeace Thackeray

———

It is something – it can be everything – to
have found a fellow bird with whom
you can sit among the rafters while
the drinking and boasting and reciting
and fighting go on below.

Wallace Stegner

———

Perhaps the feelings that we experience
when we are in love represent a normal
state. Being in love shows a person who he
should be.

Anton Chekhov

Wishing you a very happy Valentine's Day.
I'm so glad that you are mine.

———•———

I thought I knew what love was, but I was
wrong. I have never felt like this before
and I am so excited to see what our future
brings. Happy Valentine's Day. I love you.

———•———

I had given up hope that I would ever
find somebody who was perfect for me until
you walked into my life. You make me so
very happy. I love you.

———•———

Every time I look into your eyes I fall
in love again. Thank you for making every
day so exciting and full of joy. Happy
Valentine's Day.

———•———

When I'm sad you bring me joy. When
there's chaos you bring me peace. When it
rains you bring me sunshine. I'm so happy
that you are my Valentine.

Happy Valentine's Day! These last
few [weeks/months] have been the happiest
of my life. The path ahead is full of
unknowns, but I just can't wait to
travel it with you.

———•———

I feel like you and I were made for
each other and the universe always intended
for our paths to cross. I love you more than
anything. Happy Valentine's Day.

———•———

You came into my life like an angel
sent to make me whole. Every day spent
with you is the happiest of my life.
Happy Valentine's Day.

Grow old along with me!
The best is yet to be.

Robert Browning

Accept this message,
Dearest, I pray
From one who loves you,
'Tis Valentine's Day.

19th-century Valentine

I cannot exist without you. I am forgetful of everything but seeing you again – my life seems to stop there – I see no further.

John Keats

Your **words** are my **food,** your **breath** my **wine.** You are **everything** to **me.**

Sarah Bernhardt

FOR LONG-TERM PARTNERS

Even after all these years, you still take my breath away every time you smile at me. I'm so very glad I have you in my life. Happy Valentine's Day.

———

I feel like the luckiest man alive to have someone as amazing as you for my wife. Thank you for giving me a wonderful family and a wonderful home, and for bringing such happiness into my life. The years just keep getting better and better. I love you.

———

You've helped me through the rough times, been there to share in the joys, cheered me up when I've felt sad and supported me in everything I do. Thank you for being the wonderful man that you are. I love you so very much.

Some of my favourite things in this world: your incredible laugh, your soft touch, your gentle breath as we fall asleep at night. Thank you for making each and every day the happiest of my life.
I love you.

Our love is the kind of love they write songs about. Thanks for being my love, my inspiration and my very best friend every single day of our lives.
Happy Valentine's Day.

The day I married you and we began our lives together was the happiest day of my life. Each and every day since then, I've loved you more and I can no longer imagine what life was like without you.
I am so very glad that you're my Valentine.

But to see her
was to
love her,
love but her,
and love
forever.

Robert Burns

Take this token of affection.
May its beauty move thy heart.
Chill me not with cold rejection,
Bid not all my hopes depart.

19th-century Valentine

Doubt thou the stars are fire;
Doubt that the sun doth move;
Doubt truth to be a liar,
But never doubt I love.

William Shakespeare

You have turned all my winters into summers. Thank you for being my [husband/wife] and my very best friend.
Happy Valentine's Day.

———•———

It is in your arms that I find warmth, security, happiness and love. I look forward to spending many more years wrapped up in them. Happy Valentine's Day.

———•———

Despite all the things we've had to face, we've made it through and we're stronger than ever before. You're the person I want by my side always.
I love you.

———•———

The first time I ever saw you I knew you were the one for me and each and every moment we spend together is more special than the last.
Happy Valentine's Day.

I love you more than anything in this world and I can't imagine what life would be like without you. You are my everything. Happy Valentine's Day.

———•———

No gift, no matter how sweet, could ever mean as much to me as just being able to hold your hand. I love you more than anything and I look forward to being by your side for the rest of my life. Happy Valentine's Day.

———•———

I am so very thankful each and every day that I have you in my life. You uplift me; you give me the strength to be the person I want to be. I love you. Happy Valentine's Day.

———•———

You are what makes my life worth living. You are my diamond in the rough. Happy Valentine's Day. I love you.

MOTHER'S DAY AND FATHER'S DAY

You don't really understand
human
nature
unless you know
why a child on a
merry-go-round
will wave at his
parents
every time around –
and why his parents will always wave back.

William D. Tammeus

MOTHER'S DAY – FOR MOTHERS

Thank you so much for always being there for me. Thank you for the sacrifices, the love and the support. I couldn't have hoped for a better mum than you. Happy Mother's Day.

———•———

The gentlest person I will ever know is also the strongest. I love you so very much and wish you all the happiness there is to be had on Mother's Day.

———•———

You spend all of your time working hard and looking after everyone else, but today is a day for sitting back, relaxing and letting us all take care of you. Happy Mother's Day!

Hope you have a wonderful Mother's Day, Mum! Enjoy this one special day that is all about you – you deserve it.

———

Thank you for being so many things to me: a mum, a teacher, a nurse, a playmate, an inspiration. So many people come and go, but you are the one person who is always there, and I want you to know how grateful I feel to have you in my life. Happy Mother's Day.

———

Happy Mother's Day, Mum! I hope you have a fabulous day full of all those things that you give to us each and every day: fun, laughter, good food and loving family.

———

Happy Mother's Day, Mum! I'm so sorry I can't be there to spend the day with you. I am thinking of you, though, and missing you heaps. I hope you get all the pampering you deserve.

An ounce of mother is worth
a pound of priests.

Spanish proverb

———•———

As a child, the family that I had and the love
that I had from my two parents allowed me
to go ahead . . . to search and take risks,
knowing that, if I failed, I could always
come home to a family of love and support.

Tiger Woods

———•———

If you can raise a child who can take part
of your light, part of your gifts, part of what
you've taught her and run like hell, nothing
can bring you greater joy.

Goldie Hawn

Most mothers are instinctive
philosophers.

Harriet Beecher Stowe

———

Mama always had a way of explaining
things so I could understand them.

Forrest Gump

———

I know how to do anything – I'm a mom.

Roseanne Barr

Mum, thanks for a lifetime of unconditional love, support and encouragement. You sacrificed so much to make sure we had everything we could ever need, and you always did it with good grace and cheer. We love you. Happy Mother's Day.

———•———

You've always shown me what is important in life, and today, that is you! Happy Mother's Day.

———•———

Mother's Day is the day we say in words thank you for being the brilliant person you are; every other day we say it in our hearts. I feel lucky every single day that you are my mum. Have a wonderful day.

The closest friends I have made all through life have been people who also grew up close to a beloved grandmother or grandfather.

Margaret Mead

———

I think my life began with waking up and loving my mother's face.

George Eliot, **Daniel Deronda**

———

Motherhood: All love begins and ends there.

Robert Browning

A **house** needs a
grandma
in it.

Louisa May Alcott

Mother's Day – For Grandmothers

Happy Mother's Day, Gran! We hope you have a wonderful day full of all the things you love most.

———•———

You've always been a wonderful grandmother and we're so glad to have you in our lives. Thank you for everything you do for us and the way you care so much about us all. Happy Mother's Day!

———•———

Just wanted to let you know I'm thinking of you this Mother's Day and I hope you're happy, healthy and having fun. Love you, Gran!

———•———

Some of my happiest childhood memories are of big warm hugs from my Gran. I thought today was the perfect day to send some back. Happy Mother's Day!

MOTHER'S DAY – FOR PARTNERS

I am very lucky to have an extraordinary woman like you in my life. Thank you for being a beautiful wife to me and a wonderful mother to our children.
Happy Mother's Day.

———

Watching you hold our [son/daughter] in your arms makes me feel like my heart might burst with pride. The way you love [him/her], care for [him/her] and teach [him/her] is truly amazing to see. [He/She] is the world's luckiest little [boy/girl] to have you as [his/her] mum.
Happy Mother's Day.

———

I don't think there is another man in the world who loves someone as much as I love you. Thank you for giving me a beautiful family and a beautiful life. We're so lucky to have you. Happy Mother's Day.

The moment a child is born, a mother is also born. . . A mother is something absolutely new.

Bhagwan Shree Rajneesh

Nobody knows of the work it makes
To keep the home together,
Nobody knows of the steps it takes,
Nobody knows but mother.

Anonymous

A mother is the truest friend we have, when trials heavy and sudden, fall upon us; when adversity takes the place of prosperity; when friends who rejoice with us in our sunshine desert us; when trouble thickens around us, still will she cling to us, and endeavor by her kind precepts and counsels to dissipate the clouds of darkness, and cause peace to return to our hearts.

Washington Irving

You're the backbone of this family.
You're like the electrical tape that
holds the two halves of my car
together.

Homer Simpson

Things a mother should know: how to
construct a packed lunch, a shepherd's
costume and a plausible Off Games
note in ten minutes flat, usually while
cooking breakfast.

Katharine Whitehorn

FATHER'S DAY – FOR FATHERS

I've followed in your footsteps and because of you I have achieved my dreams. You are an inspiration to all, but especially to me. Thanks, Dad, for always being there for me. Happy Father's Day.

My life has been blessed because of the extraordinary person I discovered in my father. I am so proud to be your [son/ daughter]. Happy Father's Day.

To be told 'you're just like your father' is, to me, one of the great honours in life. I hope that says it all. Have a wonderful Father's Day.

To the greatest Dad a girl could ever have, happy Father's Day! I hope your day is full of all the joy you so deserve.

We just wanted to say thank you for being a great dad and a great man. Your hard work, kindness and generosity have shown us how to be the people we are today.
Happy Father's Day.

———◆———

Thank you so much for everything you do for us. You've always been our dad, our teacher, our friend and the glue that holds us all together. You've given everything you've had to your family and we just want you to know how much we appreciate it.
Happy Father's Day.

———◆———

Happy Father's Day, Dad! I am so lucky to have grown up with such a wonderful father – you've always been there to love me, support me, encourage me and cheer me on.

———◆———

May all your dreams and wishes come true on this wonderful day that is all yours.
Happy Father's Day, Dad!

You've always been my greatest inspiration. Your wisdom, your wit, your strength, your kindness, your love; I truly admire these traits that are what make you the man in life I admire the most. Happy Father's Day.

———

Thank you for being someone I could always count on. Your advice, support, honesty and encouragement have always given me the strength to dream and achieve. I hope you know how much that means to me. Happy Father's Day.

———

Thank you for always doing what was best for us, even if sometimes we didn't understand. Thank you for being strong and good and kind, and all the things a kid could ever need in a dad. Happy Father's Day.

———

When I was young, I looked up to you with admiration and respect and, now that I am an adult, nothing has changed. You'll always be the world's greatest dad. Happy Father's Day.

A father is the one friend upon whom
we can always rely. In the hour of need,
when all else fails, we remember him
upon whose knees we sat when children,
and who soothed our sorrows; and
even though he may be unable to assist
us, his mere presence serves to comfort
and strengthen us.

Émile Gaboriau, **File No. 113**

The heart of a father is the masterpiece
of nature.

Antoine François Prévost,
Manon Lescaut

A child's hand in yours – what
tenderness and power it arouses.
You are instantly the very touchstone
of wisdom and strength.

Marjorie Holmes

We never know the
love of a
parent until we
become parents
ourselves.

Henry Ward Beecher

FATHER'S DAY – FOR GRANDFATHERS

Thank you, Grandpa, for all the kindness you have shown me throughout my life, and for all the little moments we've shared. I will always cherish them. Happy Father's Day.

———

To the world's greatest Grandad: Happy Father's Day! I hope you're living it up, just like you always do.

———

Some grandparents spoil their grandkids with toys and gifts, but instead you spoiled me with your time and your love. I wouldn't swap those memories for anything in this world. Happy Father's Day, Grandpa.

———

Happy Father's Day, Grandpa. Thank you for being such an incredible role model for us and such a positive influence in our lives. We know how very lucky we are – they just don't make them like you any more.

FATHER'S DAY – FOR PARTNERS

Thank you for being there for us every day with your love and support. You are a brilliant father and a wonderful husband, and you make us all so very happy.
Have a great Father's Day.

———•———

You are an amazing dad and it makes me so proud to see the way our children adore you and know they can always count on you to make their world good and happy. Thank you for being the man that you are.
Happy Father's Day.

———•———

Thank you for being an amazing father to our beautiful little [boy/girl]. I know [he/she] will never want for anything with a father like you to love, guide, support and protect [him/her]. Happy Father's Day!

FESTIVE
OCCASIONS

Christmas waves a magic wand over this world, and behold, everything is softer and more beautiful.

Norman Vincent Peale

CHRISTMAS

May your Christmas be filled with the
love of family and the joy of friends.
We hope you all have a wonderful
holiday season.

———•———

May the magic of Christmas fill your
hearts and your home with joy today and
every day of the coming year.

———•———

Wishing you and your family all the
love, peace and joy in the world
this Christmas.

———•———

Hang the lights, pull out the stockings and
decorate the tree – it's that magical time
of year again! May your festive season be
full of joy. Merry Christmas.

Hanging stockings, wrapping gifts and spending time with those we love – what a magical time of year! Wishing you all a very merry Christmas and a safe and happy New Year.

———

We hope that Santa finds you all safe and well this Christmas. Have a wonderful holiday season!

———

We wish more than anything that we could be home with you for the holidays! We hope you and all the family are happy and healthy and that all your Christmas wishes come true!

———

Merry Christmas! May all the joy and happiness of this magical season find you, even though you're so far from home.

It is that time of year when we give thanks
for the gifts of family, friendship and love.
We hope your holiday season is full of all of
these things. Merry Christmas!

———•———

From all of us here to all of you there, we
hope your Christmas is filled with goodwill,
peace and love. Have a wonderful
holiday season!

———•———

Thank you for making every day so bright
and shiny – there is no one with whom
I would rather be sharing this special day.
I hope you have a wonderful Christmas
and I look forward to spending many more
happy Christmases together.

———•———

Merry Christmas to you on this most magical
day of the year! I hope your stocking is full,
your heart is fuller and you are surrounded
by family and friends.

To a very dear friend on a very special day, I just wanted to say thank you for all the good times and the laughs. Your friendship is the most valuable gift I could ever hope for. Have a very merry Christmas and a bright and happy New Year.

———•———

Season's greetings to you and your family at this special time of year. May you all have a happy and healthy holiday and a safe and prosperous New Year.

———•———

The holiday season is a time of year when I always think of happy times past, spent with treasured friends. Thinking of you and missing you this Christmas. I hope it is truly a wonderful one.

———•———

Thank you for being there for me at Christmas and always. I hope you have a magical holiday season. Merry Christmas.

May the joy of Christmas be yours
throughout the season, and throughout your
life. Have a wonderful day.

———

Wishing you and your family delight, peace
and prosperity this holiday season.

———

We hope you have a fun and happy
Christmas and a bright and sunny New Year.
You deserve it!

———

It's time for gathering around the
Christmas tree, sharing gifts, good food and
good company. Hope your Christmas is
full of cheer!

CHRISTMAS FOR CHILDREN

Lots of Christmas wishes and warm hugs
and kisses to a little [boy/girl] who deserves
them! We hope you have a wonderful day.

On this very special day, we wish you piles
of toys and mountains of joy! We hope
you have a magical Christmas filled with
everything that makes you smile.

Santa's coming, and I bet you just can't wait!
You're such a wonderful little [boy/girl],
I'm sure he's got something special for you!
Have a very merry Christmas and may all
your dreams come true.

Here's a special Christmas wish
That comes from us to you:
We hope your day is filled with fun
And lots of presents, too!

NEW YEAR

We just wanted to say thank you to our loyal friends for another wonderful year. May the New Year bring everything you hope for!

We're sending you our best wishes for a bright and prosperous New Year, filled with happiness for you and your family.

In the New Year, may you be blessed with everything you desire, just as we have been blessed by having two such wonderful friends.

Happy New Year! Congratulations on another incredible year. We hope that the new one will bring just as much joy and good fortune.

Write in your heart that every day is the best day of the year.

Ralph Waldo Emerson

Begin what you want to do now. We have only this moment, sparkling like a star in our hand, and melting like a snowflake.

Marie Ray

Tomorrow is the most important thing in life. Comes to us at midnight very clean. It's perfect when it arrives and it puts itself in our hands. It hopes we've learnt something from yesterday.

John Wayne

Out of Eternity the new day is born: into Eternity at night will return.

Thomas Carlyle

EASTER

Wishing you and your family a very happy Easter. May it be filled with love, laughter and happiness.

———•———

We hope the Easter Bunny found you safe and well. Have a happy Easter!

———•———

May you have an Easter filled with fun, friends, family and, most of all, chocolate! Wishing you all the best at this special time.

———•———

Easter is a very special time for families to come together and celebrate life's blessings. Wishing you all joy and happiness over this holiday period.

GRADUATION

Education is the most powerful weapon which you can use to change the world.

Nelson Mandela

Leaving School

We can't believe this day is finally here,
where you say goodbye to childhood forever
and venture out into the wide world as an
adult. We are so very proud of you, and we
can't wait to see what your bright future
holds. Congratulations on your graduation.

———•———

Congratulations on your graduation. Six long
years of hard work and dedication have
paid off and you can now look forward to
a bright and promising future. You have
made us very proud of who you are and
everything you have achieved.

———•———

Say goodbye to uniforms, classrooms,
teachers, assignments and homework.
From now on your life will be whatever you
choose to make it. Congratulations on
your graduation.

It's time to celebrate many years of hard work and be proud of all that you have achieved. We wish you all the very best as you complete this important stage of your life and begin on a new journey that we're sure will see you reach even greater heights.

———•———

It is time to say goodbye to one of life's great journeys and welcome in an even greater one. Congratulations on this momentous occasion.

———•———

It has been a pleasure to watch you grow into the incredible young [man/woman] you have become. We have every faith that you are ready to go out into the world and achieve whatever your dreams may hold. Congratulations on your graduation.

I am a woman in process. I'm just trying like everybody else. I try to take every conflict, every experience, and learn from it. Life is never dull.

Oprah Winfrey

There are no limits to growth because there are no limits to human intelligence, imagination and wonder.

Ronald Reagan

Far away in the sunshine are my highest aspirations. I may not reach them, but I can look up and see their beauty, believe in them, and try to follow where they lead.

Louisa May Alcott

———

Without leaps of imagination, or dreaming, we lose the excitement of possibilities. Dreaming, after all, is a form of planning.

Gloria Steinem

———

Those who dream by day are cognizant of many things which escape those who dream only by night.

Edgar Allan Poe

UNIVERSITY

You've finally made it to the end of a long and challenging road. Take a deep breath, reflect on all that you have achieved and celebrate! Congratulations.

———————

Today marks the end of a huge part of your life, and the beginning of an even bigger one. You have already proven that you have what it takes to make a success of anything you set out to achieve. We're so very proud of you.

———————

Biggest congratulations on your graduation. You have achieved so much for someone so young, and we wish you all the very best as you begin down this exciting new path. May life bring everything you could hope for.

———————

Congratulations on all you have achieved. The past [number] years were for studying and working hard, but today is for celebrating and receiving the rewards you so greatly deserve.

Today caps will fly and diplomas will
be handed out in honour of a great
achievement. We are so happy to be here on
this day sharing in the joy of your success.

If you can confront all the challenges ahead
with the same tenacity and flair that you
have shown in your past accomplishments,
the future is yours for the taking.

We couldn't be any prouder of you
than we are today on your graduation.
It has been a pleasure to watch you grow
into the [man/woman] you have become:
a true and loyal friend, a hard-working and
gifted student, and a warm and generous
person. Congratulations.

My philosophy of life is that if we make up our minds what we are going to make of our lives, then work hard toward that goal, we never lose – somehow we win out.

Ronald Reagan

What would you attempt if you knew you could not fail?

Robert H. Schuller

All successful people have a goal. No one can get anywhere unless he knows where he wants to go and what he wants to be or do.

Norman Vincent Peale

Intellectual growth should commence at birth and cease only at death.

Albert Einstein

———•———

Women are always being tested . . . but ultimately, each of us has to define who we are individually and then do the very best we can to grow into that.

Hillary Clinton

———•———

Examine myself as I may, I can no longer find the slightest trace of the anxious, agitated individual of those years, so discontented with herself, so out of patience with others.

George Sand

Apprenticeships and Traineeships

Today you reap the rewards of what has taken years of dedication to achieve. We offer you our sincerest congratulations on completing your apprenticeship.

After much hard work and dedication, you have now achieved your dream of becoming a [occupation]. We are sure that you'll prove to be a huge success.

We know it was often tough and sometimes it felt like you would never reach the end, but you stuck with it and have finally achieved that long sought-after goal. We admire your determination and are very proud of what you have achieved. Well done.

It is time now to enjoy all that you have achieved. Congratulations.

Throw your dreams
into space
like a kite,
and you do not know what
they will bring
back –
a new life, a new friend,
a new love, a new
country.

Anais Nin

Shoot for the moon. Even if you miss it you will land among the stars.

Les Brown

———•———

Set your sights high, the higher the better. Expect the most wonderful things to happen, not in the future but right now. Realise that nothing is too good. Allow absolutely nothing to hamper you or hold you up in any way.

Eileen Caddy

Congratulations on the completion of your traineeship. You created a plan, worked hard, strived against the odds and pushed through to the very end. We're very proud.

The path to success was full of challenges but you persevered and made it. Enjoy your wonderful achievements.

Congratulations on completing your apprenticeship. You overcame each challenge, demand and trial that life set before you with quiet grace. All your hard work has finally paid off and now you can take some time to enjoy your success.

May your future be filled with many successes and happy tomorrows. Congratulations on this wonderful achievement.

ACHIEVEMENTS

It is not the mountain we conquer but ourselves.

Sir Edmund Hillary

GENERAL

You've worked so hard to achieve your dreams and now it's time to enjoy your successes. Congratulations.

———•———

Congratulations on this great achievement. You are an inspiration to us all and you should be immensely proud of your success.

———•———

Congratulations on all you have achieved. You deserve it.

———•———

Congratulations! You're living proof that anything can be achieved through hard work and dedication.

———•———

The journey to success was long and often hard, but you never lost sight of your dreams. Congratulations.

New Job

Congratulations on your new job. You've worked so hard to achieve your dreams and now it's time to reap the benefits of your hard work. Enjoy the path of success.

We watched with pride as you strived to reach your goals. We couldn't be prouder of you and all you have achieved. Congratulations.

You've made it! All the years of study and hard work have now paid off. Congratulations on this exciting new journey, and may it be just the beginning of a successful and fulfilling career.

Congratulations on landing the dream job. I hope that it is everything you wish it to be, and I'm sure you'll give it everything you've got!

I am thankful to all those who said 'No' to me. It's because of them I'm doing it myself.

Albert Einstein

It is a common experience that a problem which is difficult at night is resolved in the morning after the committee of sleep has worked on it.

John Steinbeck

Life affords no higher pleasure than that of surmounting difficulties, passing from one step of success to another, forming new wishes and seeing them gratified.

Samuel Johnson

No **bird** soars

too **high** if he

soars with

his **own** wings.

William Blake

PROMOTION

You accepted the challenge, fought hard
to succeed and now you've made it!
Congratulations on your promotion.

———•———

Congratulations on the big promotion! We
hope your future is filled with as many
successes as you've already achieved.

———•———

You dreamt, you persevered, you achieved.
Well done!

———•———

We always knew that others would see
in you the same qualities that we do:
intellect, initiative, imagination, dedication,
enthusiasm. We are so very proud of all
your hard work. Congratulations on this
wonderful achievement.

———•———

Congratulations! No person deserves this
success more than you. Enjoy it.

In everyone there is something precious, found in no one else; so honour each man for what is hidden within him – for what he alone has, and none of his fellows.

Hasidic saying

I still find each day too short for all the thoughts I want to think, all the walks I want to take, all the books I want to read, and all the friends I want to see.

John Burroughs

———•———

No longer forward nor behind
I look in hope and fear;
But grateful for the good I find,
The best of now and here.

John G. Whittier

Awards

When you set your goals so high the achievement is so much more rewarding. Congratulations on reaching the sky.

———•———

It is only when we give disregard to the possibility of failure that we can achieve great things. It is wonderful to see you so justly rewarded for your vision, hard work and dedication.

———•———

Making something possible depends not on what others believe of you, but what you believe of yourself. You have certainly proved that you can do anything you set your mind to. Congratulations.

———•———

We are so very proud of the great things you have achieved and the difference you have made to people's lives along the way. You deserve this great honour.

GOODBYE AND GOOD LUCK

Promise

me you'll never

forget me

because if

I thought you

would I'd never

leave.

Winnie the Pooh

Leaving a Job

Wishing you happiness and success in your new job. We're going to miss you!

———◆———

What are we going to do without you? Who's going to look after us, keep our spirits up and, most importantly, fix the photocopier?! We're so sad that you're leaving, but we wish you joy and luck as you begin your new adventure.

———◆———

Congratulations on your new job! We hope they realise how lucky they are to have you onboard. We wish you the very best of luck and look forward to catching up soon.

———◆———

Goodbye and good luck! We wish you and your family all the very best for the future. Keep in touch.

We'd like to take this opportunity to thank you for all your years of hard work with [company] and for all the contributions you have made. We know you'll make a success of this new job just as you made a success of your role here. Best wishes for the future.

———•———

It has been a pleasure working with you over the last [number] years, and I'll miss seeing your sunny face around the office. Best wishes for the future. I hope it brings you all the happiness you deserve.

———•———

So sad to be saying goodbye! We wish you weren't leaving us but we hope your new opportunity proves to be everything you've hoped for. Good luck, [name], we'll miss you!

Never underestimate the power of dreams and the influence of the human spirit. We are all the same in this notion: the potential for greatness lives within each of us.

Wilma Rudolph

———•———

All big men are dreamers. They see things in the soft haze of a spring day or in the red fire of a long winter's evening. Some of us let great dreams die, but others nourish and protect them, nurse them through bad days till they bring them into the sunshine and light which comes always to those who sincerely hope that their dreams will come true.

Woodrow Wilson

Do the thing you fear and the death of fear is certain.

Ralph Waldo Emerson

Retirement

You've put in so many years of hard work and now it's time to sit back, relax and enjoy the sunshine. Congratulations on your retirement!

Congratulations on your retirement! Your career has been a long and successful one, full of triumphs and achievements. You've given so much to [the company/industry] and you have truly earned the right to walk away proud of all you have accomplished. Best wishes to you and [name of partner] as you begin this exciting new time in your lives.

Congratulations on your retirement. After [number] years of hard work, you certainly deserve it! We hope you will now be able to find the time to do the things you've always dreamed about. Good luck!

You must be very proud as you reflect back on a lifetime of hard work, challenges and success. You have more than earned this opportunity to take some time just for yourself and your family, and we wish you every happiness for this new phase of your life.

———•———

Congratulations on taking the plunge and jumping into the most exciting stage of your life yet! The hard work is all behind you and the fun is just about to start. Best wishes for a happy retirement.

———•———

Congratulations on your retirement! A life of reading reports, attending meetings and working late has now become a life of reading books, attending barbeques and sleeping late! Enjoy this wonderful time of your life, you have truly earned it.

Moving Away

We're so sad that you're leaving! Best of luck with the move and your new home, and we hope this adventure is everything you dream it will be. I hope we'll see you again soon.

After having you so close by for so long, I don't know what I'm going to do without you! I wish you the very best of everything life can bring in your new home. Keep in touch!

Wishing you the best of luck and sincere congratulations on this exciting opportunity – but we're really going to miss having you around! Please just let us know if we can help in any way at all.

Wishing you the best of everything in your new house, new town and new life. Goodbye and good luck!

Even though we'll be far from each other in person, we'll always be close in spirit. Remember that I'm always here, just a phone call or a short flight away. I'm really going to miss you!

We know that you'll find every happiness in your new life in [place], and we look forward to being able to come and visit sometime soon to see it for ourselves. We'll miss you!

Saying goodbye to good friends is always hard, but we know this isn't the end – it's just the beginning of an exciting new adventure. Just remember that we'll always be here. We'll miss you so very much.

I can't believe it's time to say goodbye! I know you'll create a happy and wonderful life for yourselves in [place], with new experiences and many new friends. I'll be thinking of you!

Life **shrinks** or expands in proportion to **one's** courage.

Anais Nin

You are never too old to set another goal or to dream a new dream.

C.S. Lewis

Going on a Journey

We're so excited that you're going on this grand adventure and you'll have the opportunity to see and experience things that some people can only dream of. But while you're out there seeing the big wide world, don't forget there are people here who love you and are only a phone call away. We'll miss you more than we can say.

I can't believe you're really going! You must be so very excited to be going on this wonderful adventure. Make sure you take really good care of yourself and send postcards whenever you can. Have a blast!

Wishing you all the very best as you begin your exciting journey. Be careful, have fun, and we look forward to catching up and hearing all about it when you return.

Go confidently in the direction of your dreams. Live the life you have imagined.

Henry David Thoreau

Travelling–it leaves you speechless, then turns you into a storyteller.

Ibn Battuta

We're all born under the same sky, but we don't all have the same horizons.

Konrad Adenauer

One can never consent to creep when one feels an impulse to soar.

Helen Keller

Wishing you a wonderful holiday – and I hope it's everything you've been dreaming of. Look after each other, stay safe, and come home happy and healthy. I'm so very jealous!

Wishing you an exciting year full of different cultures, new experiences and adventure. You've worked very hard to deserve this trip – make the most of it! Congratulations and good luck.

Good luck on your travels! I have heard that [place] is a wonderful place and I can't wait to see your photos and hear your stories when you come home. I'll be thinking of you while you're gone.

Eat lots of food, have lots of fun and make lots of friends but, most importantly of all, come home safe! Hope your holiday is a wonderful adventure. We will miss you very much.

GET WELL SOON

The
best
of
healers
is good
cheer.

Pindar

Minor Illness

Get well soon, [name]! We all miss you very much and hope you'll be back on your feet in no time.

———•———

Just writing to let you know that we're thinking of you and hoping for a speedy recovery. Get well soon.

———•———

We were very glad to hear that your [operation/procedure] went well. Here's hoping for a strong and quick recovery – it's just not the same here without you.

———•———

We were so sorry to hear of your recent illness. Make sure you take all the time you need to rest, relax and recover. Get well soon!

Sending you a thousand smiles to brighten your day. Get well soon.

———•———

We were very surprised and concerned to hear of your recent accident. We're so glad that you are okay and hope you'll be feeling one hundred per cent again soon.

———•———

Just letting you know that we're thinking of you. Rest, stay strong and get better soon. Please let us know if we can help in any way.

———•———

We know being sick isn't very much fun, but we hope that sunshine and blue skies come your way soon.

———•———

Sometimes when you're unwell it helps to know that people are thinking of you and hoping that you'll get better soon. Take good care of yourself.

Major Illness

We were so very sorry to hear that you haven't been well. We hope that you'll feel better very soon. Our thoughts and wishes are with you.

———•———

We know you're strong enough to beat this – and we'll always be here if you ever need a helping hand. If there is anything we can do to help please just let us know.

———•———

You're always taking care of everybody else, but now it's time to let us take care of you. We'll be here to love and support you every step of the way, and we look forward to having you fit and strong again soon.

———•———

Our thoughts are with you and your family during this difficult time. We are all hoping and wishing that happier, healthier days are coming your way.

We've all been thinking of you and
what a hard time you must be going through
at the moment. We hope our heartfelt wishes
and loving thoughts can add some cheer
to your day.

———

We're so proud of your strength and
determination. It is a true inspiration to
us all to see how you face every day with
spirit and courage. We're so sorry you're
going through this awful time, but please
remember that we'll be right here whenever
you need us.

———

I was very sorry to hear of your illness.
I know times must be hard right now
but I'm sure it will be no time at all before
you're up and about and doing all the
things you love once again.

———

Thinking of you during this terrible time.
We hope with all of our hearts that you will
get well soon.

Just wanted to let you know I've been thinking about you and everything you're going through. Hope you'll be feeling like your old self again soon.

———•———

I know you must be feeling scared and anxious right now and I wish there was something I could do to make you feel better. I hope you'll have some good news soon but, in the meantime, don't forget that I'm here for whatever it is you need.

———•———

I wish there was something more I could do to help you through this terrible time. Just remember that I will always be here to give you friendship, support, a shoulder to cry on and a hand to hold.

Comedy is defiance. It's a snort of contempt
in the face of fear and anxiety. And it's the
laughter that allows hope to creep back on
the inhale.

Will Durst

The only courage that matters
is the kind that gets you from one
moment to the next.

Mignon McLaughlin

It does not matter how slowly you go,
as long as you do not stop.

Confucius

The bravest thing you can do when you
are not brave is to profess courage and
act accordingly.

Corra May White Harris

Disease is war with the laws of our
being, and all war, as a great general
has said, is hell.

Lewis G. Janes

FOR CHILDREN

Even though you can't see them, this card is full of happy thoughts and big hugs to help you get better soon.

Oh, no! How terrible that you've been sick. We're all thinking of you and hope you get your sparkle back real soon.

We're so sorry you haven't been feeling well! You've been such a brave little [boy/girl] and we hope that you feel much better soon.

We're sorry you're sick,
It makes us sad.
Get well real quick!
Love Mum and Dad.

SYMPATHY

Is it so
small a thing
to have enjoyed the sun,
To have
lived light
in the spring,
To have loved,
to have thought, to have
done...

Matthew Arnold

GENERAL

It is during times of great loss that we realise how limiting words can be and how special our friends truly are. We hope you hear the words we cannot speak, for words can do no justice to the heartache you and your family have suffered. We ask that you don't mourn the loss of [name] alone and that you share your memories of [him/her] with us.

———•———

Our hearts and thoughts are with you during this time of grieving. Please know that you are not alone in remembering a truly wonderful person that meant so much to so many.

———•———

Please know that we are mourning with you the loss of [name], who was a very dear friend. We find comfort in the knowledge that [his/her] kindness, compassion and spirit will live on through those [he/she] has left behind.

Try to remember the little things, the shared smiles, the warm hugs, the laughter. The pain might seem unbearable now, but in time, it is these memories that will win through and you will find happiness again. Our thoughts are with you.

———•———

Our deepest sympathies are with you during this time of loss. We hope you can find reassurance in the care of your friends, and allow the loving memories you have of [name] to help you through this time.

———•———

Our sincerest sympathies are with you during this difficult time. Your mother was a wonderful woman, full of strength and goodness. She will be sorely missed.

———•———

Please accept my sincerest condolences on the passing of your dad. He will always be remembered as a hard-working, honest and respectable man, and a great father. My thoughts are with you and your family.

Sometimes it's hard not to wish for one more day, one more word, one more chance to say goodbye, but you should rest assured that you were a joy to your [mum/dad] every day of your life and [he/she] was immensely proud of you. It was a privilege to have known [him/her] and we can see that [his/her] goodness lives on through you and your family.

———•———

Please accept my deepest condolences for your loss. Please don't hesitate to let me know if there's anything I can do for you or your family during this very difficult time.

———•———

I know at times like this it is hard to see past the sorrow, but I hope that reflecting on the wonderful memories that you and [name] shared will help you to see light again. My deepest sympathies for your loss.

UNEXPECTED LOSS

The sudden loss of [name] was a shock to
us all. Please know you are not alone as you
face the daunting path of grief and mourning.
We cannot remove the heartache you're
suffering but we can and will surround you
with love and support, every step of the way.

———•———

During times of loss we find ourselves
troubled by things we do not understand.
There are no answers to comfort your grief,
only lasting love and precious memories. We
are thinking of you during this sad time.

———•———

We were so sorry to hear of the tragic passing
of [name]. Please know that you can lean on
us for strength during this difficult time, and
remember that we will always be here.

The more enriched a person makes our lives, the harder it is for us to let them go. For this reason, I know that saying goodbye to [name] will be the hardest sorrow to bear. I hope that the wonderful memories you have of [name], as well as the love and friendship you have around you, will support you through this time and help you to smile once more.

———•———

Words seem inadequate to express the sadness we feel at the tragic loss of [name]. Our hearts go out to you and your family in your time of sorrow.

———•———

I just wanted to tell you how surprised and saddened I was to hear of the passing of [name]. [He/she] always seemed so happy and full of life. Please extend my sympathy to your family and know that I am thinking of you all at this sorrowful time.

LOSS AFTER ILLNESS

We are very saddened by the passing of [name], but we know [he/she] is now truly at peace. We know this must be a very difficult time for you and your family, but please feel that you can reach out to us for anything you may need.

———◆———

It seems so very hard to believe that [name] is gone, even though [he/she] had been sick for such a long time. Please remember that we will always be right here with you to remember, reminisce, cry and laugh. We will miss [him/her] so very much.

———◆———

[Name's] life was a life lived to its fullest. A happy marriage, a wonderful family and a loving home were just some of the great things [he/she] accomplished. With so many children, grandchildren and great-grandchildren, [his/her] legacy will certainly live on.

SAYING SORRY

The
ability
of a person to
atone
has always been the
most remarkable of
human
features.

Leon Uris

TO A PARTNER

I'm so very sorry for all the things I didn't say and do when you really needed me. Please forgive me.

Please forgive me if what I [did/said] upset you. I never meant to hurt you and it breaks my heart to think that I have made you sad. I'm really sorry.

I am deeply sorry that I hurt you. I know just these words can't make things right, but I want you to know how much I regret what I did to make you sad. I love you with all my heart and hope that you will let me make it up to you.

I don't expect forgiveness, I just want you to know that you didn't deserve what happened between us. I am sincerely sorry.

It is my job to bring sunshine into your life,
and instead I brought a storm. I promise
I will try to make it up to you a thousand
times over.

———•———

I am sorry that I couldn't be there for your
[occasion]. Even though you've been so
understanding, I wish more than anything
I could have been there to share it with you.
I'll make it up to you in any way I can.

———•———

You are the one thing in my life that I am
supposed to love, protect and value above
all else. I'll try my very best to make sure
I never lose sight of what's important again.
I'm so very sorry I let you down.

To keep your marriage brimming
With love in the wedding cup,
Whenever you're wrong admit it;
Whenever you're right, shut up.

Ogden Nash

The ultimate test of a relationship
is to disagree but hold hands.

Alexandra Penney

Never forget the nine most important
words of any family –
I love you.
You are beautiful.
Please forgive me.

H. Jackson Brown Jr.

Life is to be
fortified
by many
friendships.
To love and to be
loved is the
greatest happiness
in existence.

Sydney Smith

To a Friend

I'm so very sorry that we argued [when].
Please believe me when I say that I didn't
mean the hurtful things I said. Your
friendship means a lot to me and I hope that
you can forgive me.

———•———

I just wanted to say I'm sorry. I see now that
I was wrong and I have treated you unfairly.
Please accept my sincerest apologies for the
hurt that I have caused you.

———•———

I'm very sorry if I have done something to
hurt you. I can feel that things aren't right
and I really hope that we can sort it out.
Our friendship is too important to lose.

———•———

I'm so sorry things turned out the way that
they did. I wish more than anything that
I had been a better friend. I miss you.

Forsake not an old friend; for the new is not comparable to him: a new friend is as new wine; when it is old, thou shalt drink it with pleasure.

Ecclesiasticus 9:10

———

A person who seeks help for a friend, while in need himself, will be answered first.

The Talmud

———

Anger is a wind which blows out the lamp of the mind.

Robert G. Ingersoll

From quiet home and first beginning,
Out to undiscovered ends,
There's nothing worth the wear of winning,
But laughter and the love of friends.

Hilaire Belloc

———•———

Close friends contribute to our personal growth. They also contribute to our personal pleasure, making the music sound sweeter, the wine taste richer, the laughter ring louder because they are there.

Judith Viorst

I just wanted to get in touch and say I'm sorry it's been so long since we've spoken. Sometimes it's easy to get carried away with our own lives, but I do hope that we can catch up sometime soon.

———•———

I'm very sorry for the hurt and embarrassment I caused you. You are a good friend and a good person, and you didn't deserve my tactless [words/actions]. I hope you can find it in your heart to forgive me.

———•———

Please accept my deepest apologies for the way I behaved [when]. I regret the way I handled things and would absolutely do it differently if I had the chance again. I really do appreciate what a great friend you have been to me.

IMPORTANT DATES

For every minute spent in organising, an hour is earned.

Unknown

JANUARY

Name	Occasion	Date

FEBRUARY

Name	Occasion	Date

MARCH

Name	Occasion	Date

APRIL

Name	Occasion	Date

MAY

Name	Occasion	Date

JUNE

Name	Occasion	Date

JULY

Name	Occasion	Date

AUGUST

Name	Occasion	Date

September

Name	Occasion	Date

OCTOBER

Name	Occasion	Date

NOVEMBER

Name	Occasion	Date

DECEMBER

Name	Occasion	Date

CHRISTMAS CARD LIST

Name	Address

CHRISTMAS CARD LIST

Name	Address

NOTES

NOTES